LORETTA LYNCH

LORETTA LYNCH

FIRST AFRICAN AMERICAN WOMAN ATTORNEY GENERAL

ERIC BRAUN

LERNER PUBLICATIONS ◆ MINNEAPOLIS

Lerner Publications Company
A division of Lerner Publishing Group, Inc.
241 First Avenue North
Minneapolis, MN USA 55401

For reading levels and more information, look up this title at www.lernerbooks.com.

Main body text set in Rotis Serif Std 55 Regular 13.5/17. Typeface provided by Adobe Systems.

Library of Congress Cataloging-in-Publication Data

Braun, Eric, author.
    Loretta Lynch : first African American woman Attorney General / Eric Braun.
        pages cm
    Includes bibliographical references and index.
        ISBN 978-1-5124-0586-6 (lb : alk. paper) — ISBN 978-1-5124-0587-3 (eb pdf)
        1. Lynch, Loretta, 1959– —Juvenile literature. 2. African American women lawyers—Biography—Juvenile literature. 3. African American public prosecutors—Biography—Juvenile literature. 4. Women attorneys general—United States—Biography—Juvenile literature. I. Title.
    KF373.L95B73 2016
    349.73092—dc23 [B]   2015025914

Manufactured in the United States of America
1 – VP – 12/31/15

CONTENTS

Loretta Lynch is sworn in during her confirmation hearing in the Senate Judiciary Committee.

It was barely dawn when the dozen or so men barged into the quiet hotel lobby. Dressed in jeans, sweatshirts, and sneakers, they looked very much out of place at the Baur au Lac, one of the fanciest hotels in the world. Located in Zurich, Switzerland, this 170-year-old luxury property overlooks the Alps and beautiful Lake Zurich. Suites here can cost as much as $4,000 a night. Rather than jeans and sneakers, most guests wore dressy, expensive clothing. What were these men doing here?

Carrying green folders with lists of names, they approached the startled desk clerks and showed their badges. They were police officers, here to arrest some of the richest and most powerful people in sports—vice presidents and other high-ranking officials in FIFA (Fédération Internationale de Football Association). The organization governs soccer tournaments around the world. The officials were in town for committee meetings.

Once the officers got the room numbers they needed, they fanned out through the hotel. They found the suspects,

Police officers arrested FIFA officials at the Baur au Lac, a luxury hotel in Zurich, Switzerland.

led them out of their rooms without handcuffs, and took them outside without a struggle. Members of the media had gathered to take photos. Hotel staff—still trying to help their wealthy customers—held up white bedsheets to block the photographers' view as the officials were filed into waiting cars.

Loretta Lynch was not in Zurich that morning. She was in Brooklyn, New York, about 4,000 miles (6,437 kilometers) away. Yet she stood at the center of these arrests. She had begun investigating the FIFA officials years earlier, when she was the US attorney for the Eastern District of

New York. Now she was the US attorney general, which made her the head of the US Department of Justice and the top government law officer and lawyer.

Baur au Lac employees use sheets to conceal the FIFA officials arrested at their hotel.

A few hours after the arrests, Lynch stepped to a podium to give a speech in front of news crews with microphones and flashing cameras. Only 5 feet (1.5 meters) tall, she spoke with a calm authority amid the chaos. She explained that the charges against the officials involved "corruption that is rampant, systemic, and deep-rooted both abroad and here in the United States." She said the corruption spanned two generations and affected "a multitude of victims" that included youth leagues, developing countries that should have benefited from FIFA's revenue, and fans.

"They were expected to uphold the rules that keep soccer honest," she said of the nine top FIFA officials and five marketing executives. "Instead they corrupted the business of worldwide soccer to serve their interests and enrich themselves." A total of forty-seven corruption charges were being filed against the men.

Lynch speaks at a news conference regarding the arrest of the FIFA officials.

Lynch's speech played on news stations and websites around the world. The arrests became a sensational international story—and Lynch became a hero. Most soccer fans knew FIFA officials had been corrupt. They took millions of dollars in bribes to determine where the World Cup would be held, who would get marketing deals, and more. But it was hard to believe anyone in the organization would pay a penalty for their actions. It seemed to many that FIFA's power protected it from punishment.

Yet FIFA did face serious consequences that day in May 2015—thanks to a long investigation led by the FBI and Loretta Lynch. Since soccer is the most popular sport in the world and since the corruption within FIFA had been harming the game for so long, Lynch was praised widely. "Soccer has a new hero," one reporter wrote, adding that Lynch would "go down as the most consequential woman in the history of the game."

Lynch had been the attorney general for only a month at the time. But already she was known for going after the biggest, most hard-to-catch criminals. As a top US attorney, she had prosecuted organized crime, terrorists, sex traffickers, corrupt banks, and more. One of the first things she'd done as attorney general was to launch a major investigation into the Baltimore Police Department to determine if officers were violating the rights of citizens there. She had a reputation for being tough, determined, and fair. She fought for those who didn't have the power to fight for themselves. When President Barack Obama nominated her as attorney general, he noted that she may be the only lawyer in the country who took on powerful criminals such as mobsters and drug lords and yet was known for being charming and a "people person."

She was also the first black woman to hold this position—an achievement that did not come easily. After Obama nominated Lynch, the US Senate had to vote to confirm her. But due to political disagreements between Obama's Democratic Party and the Republicans, the confirmation was delayed for more than five months. Yet just as she did with FIFA and countless other cases, Lynch settled in for the long fight. Meanwhile, she didn't stop working. She continued to pursue the FIFA case, which she'd opened years ago based on a tip from the FBI. It was always her way to work hard and not give up.

Lynch's big payoff came on April 27, 2015. On that day,

she officially became the first African American woman to be named to the highest law office in the land—a watershed event that will go down in the history of US politics and the world.

BORN TO FIGHT FOR JUSTICE

Loretta Lynch was born on May 21, 1959, in Greensboro, North Carolina. This hilly city is nestled between the Blue Ridge and Great Smoky Mountains. Loretta grew up with an older brother, Lorenzo, and a younger brother, Leonzo. Her family's ancestors were former slaves who had made their way to the area from slave plantations.

A few months after Loretta was born, Greensboro became the heart of the civil rights movement. In February 1960, four black college students sat down at an all-white lunch counter and refused to move when they

Sit-ins were a common form of protest in the United States during the 1960s.

Lynch's mother, Lorine, and her father, Lorenzo

were denied service. Soon other people joined the "sit-in." Similar protests quickly spread across the South.

Loretta's father, Lorenzo Lynch Sr., was a Baptist minister. He opened his church basement to college students and black leaders to plan for more protests. He would carry little Loretta on his shoulders to these meetings.

Her mother, a librarian named Lorine, also believed fiercely in equality. When the family drove around rural North Carolina on preaching trips, her mother refused to use segregated restrooms. One summer she worked picking cotton so she could pay for her college education. When Loretta heard this, she asked why her mother would do a job that used to be done by slaves. Her mom replied, "So that you never have to."

Growing up in this time of racial struggle, Loretta began to learn how important it was to fight for justice. Her father told her stories about when he was growing up—when the country still had Jim Crow laws.

Though slavery was outlawed in the United States following the Civil War (1861–1865), Jim Crow laws put in place after the war segregated and discriminated against black citizens. There were separate public schools, public transportation, restrooms, restaurants, and even drinking fountains for whites and blacks. The facilities for blacks were almost always of lower quality. Black people faced discrimination in every part of public life, and if they violated Jim Crow laws—or even if a white person *said* they did—they could be tried without a jury and often faced punishment.

Under Jim Crow laws, black citizens had to use separate bathrooms from whites in some parts of the United States.

Many of the stories Loretta's father told her were about his own dad—Loretta's grandfather. He was a sharecropper. He paid a portion of his crops as rent to the white landowners who let him use their land for farming. Like his father and grandfather—and like his son would become—Loretta's grandfather was a Baptist minister. He built a church to hold services right next to his house. And inside his house, underneath the floorboards, he built a place to hide African Americans who had been accused of breaking Jim Crow laws. When the sheriff came around looking for those he was hiding, he would say he hadn't seen them—even though he risked his own life by doing so.

Hearing stories about her grandfather had a powerful effect on Loretta. She later said, "I realized the power the law had over your life and how important it was that the people who wield that power look at each situation with a sense of fairness and evenhandedness."

SCHOOL DAYS

When Loretta was six, her family moved to Durham, North Carolina. There she registered for school with black and white students. But when Loretta took a test and did better than everyone else, her teachers thought she had cheated. They couldn't believe a black student could do better than white students. Her mother fought back, saying that the school wouldn't have questioned the test score if Loretta were white. In the end, Loretta retook the test, and she did even better.

In Durham her father often took her with him to watch court proceedings. In spite of the Jim Crow laws and poor treatment blacks had received in his lifetime, her father believed law was important. He believed it could be a force for positive change.

Her father felt so strongly about the power of the law that in 1973 he ran for mayor of Durham. Loretta, who was fourteen years old, helped his campaign by stuffing envelopes and answering phones. He lost, but Loretta never forgot her first exposure to politics.

At home, Loretta spent much of her time reading. Her librarian mother filled their house with books, and Loretta devoured them. Neighbors said they often saw her walking to and from the library, a block from her home, with stacks of books in her arms.

As Loretta got older, she continued to do very well in school. She participated in the Beta Club, an academic honors group, and after school, she worked at a fast-food restaurant. She was also a talented seamstress and made outfits for herself and sometimes for her mother for special occasions.

Loretta began to think about her future. She thought getting out of the South, where minorities continued to be oppressed in many ways, might be best for her career. When she traveled with her family to Boston, Massachusetts, she saw something that affected her deeply—Harvard University, the oldest and one of the most prestigious schools in the country. She told her family she wanted to go there.

When Loretta graduated from high school in 1977, she was the top student in her class. She was the obvious choice to be valedictorian, an honor usually given to a graduating class's highest-achieving academic student. The valedictorian typically gives a speech at the class's graduation ceremony. But administrators at Durham High School had her share the honor with two others, including a white student. Administrators were nervous about the controversy they might face if they had a lone black valedictorian. The two other students were friends of Loretta, and she accepted the plan.

When it was time to choose a college, Loretta turned down a full scholarship from a college in North Carolina. Instead, she followed her dream and left home—for Harvard.

Lynch left North Carolina to attend Harvard University.

A RISING PROSECUTOR

Because she had always loved literature, Loretta Lynch majored in English at Harvard University, and she continued to be highly focused on academics. One of her favorite authors was Geoffrey Chaucer, the fourteenth-century poet who wrote *The Canterbury Tales*, which she read in the difficult Middle English of his time.

At Harvard, Lynch met Sharon Malone, a fellow African American southern woman, and the two became good friends. Lynch and Malone worked together to found a chapter of Delta Sigma Theta, a sorority for black women. People who got to know Lynch at Harvard quickly saw that she was a hard worker and stayed out of trouble. They thought of her as a "PK," or preacher's kid—a term often used to describe ministers' kids who are conscientious and tend to follow rules. Though most college students dressed casually, in jeans and T-shirts, Lynch always dressed sharply. A friend teased her, "Do you . . . have any play clothes?"

After graduating, Lynch realized that she wanted to work in law. She continued on at Harvard in the law school. Soon she began looking for a job. Once, when she arrived at a law firm for an interview, the receptionist didn't understand what she was doing there. She couldn't believe a black woman was a job candidate from Harvard.

Lynch eventually landed a job at Cahill Gordon & Reindel, a law firm in New York. One of her Harvard friends, Annette Gordon-Reed, was also hired there. Those two and a third woman were the only African

American women at the firm. The receptionists knew the names of all the 250 male lawyers working there, but they couldn't seem to tell the three black women apart. Though the new employees must have been frustrated by the way the three black women had been lumped together, they didn't show any anger. Instead, they made a joke out of it, calling themselves "the triplets," as if they really were identical.

Lynch became especially close with Gordon-Reed, who, like her, was from the South. They would share traditional southern meals on Friday nights. Mostly, though, they worked "very, very hard," said Gordon-Reed.

Lynch worked so hard, in fact, that she didn't take good care of herself. One morning a secretary found her passed out at her desk. Lynch was taken to the hospital, where she was diagnosed with exhaustion. Lying in the hospital bed with an IV drip in her arm, Lynch began to rethink her career. Was this what she really wanted to do? Could her talents be put to better use elsewhere? Was she happy?

The answer to the last question was "no." So in 1990, Lynch took a job as an assistant US attorney for the Eastern District of New York in Brooklyn. The office was not fancy. Fifteen attorneys had to share two computers. But it was there that Lynch began to find her true calling, pursuing and prosecuting criminals. She worked on cases having to do with narcotics, guns, and organized crime. She considered working on behalf of the public to be a more meaningful occupation than her former job.

In 1994 Lynch was promoted to chief of the Long Island office of the district. She worked on several political corruption cases involving the government of Brookhaven, New York. She did not back down from any fight for fairness, even against powerful politicians.

TURNING POINT

Then, in August 1997, something happened in a Brooklyn police station that would change Lynch's life forever. A thirty-year-old Haitian immigrant named Abner Louima had gone to see his favorite band at a club in Brooklyn where many Haitians liked to hang out. Sometime after three in the morning, a big fight erupted in the club, and

Abner Louima

two hundred people spilled into the street. As a couple of police officers pulled up in a squad car, Louima was trying to break up a fight between two women.

In the chaotic scene, with fighting and yelling all around, one of the officers got into an argument with Louima. The officer, Justin Volpe, was furious, perhaps about being hit during the brawl. Louima was arrested. Once Louima was in handcuffs, Volpe and other police officers beat him severely. His teeth were broken, and his eyes were swollen shut. When they got him to the police station, the police took him into a filthy public bathroom and sexually assaulted him with the handle of a toilet plunger. Louima suffered a ruptured bladder and colon and spent two months in a hospital.

Justin Volpe (*right*) is escorted from the courtroom during the Louima case.

Lynch's office was assigned to prosecute the police officers. By then she had been promoted again. She was the chief assistant to the US attorney in Brooklyn. Louima's case became a national story and the first high-profile case of Lynch's career. The violence Louima had suffered came to symbolize the police brutality people had been complaining about in New York and all around the country. Many people were outraged. Thousands of protesters marched in Brooklyn. Because the officers were white and Louima was black, the case also sparked racial tension in the city and nationwide. With the whole country watching, the scrutiny and pressure to convict the police officers were intense.

Once again, Lynch worked hard, staying at the office all hours of the day. She appeared to stay behind the scenes, allowing a junior prosecutor on the team to deliver the important opening statement for the case. When the defense mentioned that one of the officers had a black girlfriend, implying that it showed he wouldn't purposely hurt a black man, Lynch stepped in. She said the officer was "hiding behind the color of his girlfriend's skin." That statement made some officers in the audience very angry, and she had to leave the courtroom protected by guards.

Lynch had a calm but razor-sharp demeanor in the courtroom. Her tactical questioning and polished, powerful closing arguments helped her team successfully prosecute four officers. Volpe received a thirty-year prison sentence. Afterward, the US attorney for whom Lynch worked, Zachary Carter, called her "the soul of grace under pressure."

Suddenly Lynch, who had always stayed out of the spotlight, saw her name in the news. Because of her success in the Louima case, she was beginning to be noticed—even by President Bill Clinton.

A PUBLIC SERVANT

In the wake of the Louima case, Lynch's office began investigating the New York City Police Department's brutality cases. Through the investigation, Lynch and her boss, Zachary Carter, found that the NYPD often used excessive force against citizens.

During the investigation, Carter retired. President Bill Clinton chose Lynch to take over as the US attorney for the Eastern District of New York. As with many federally appointed jobs, the nomination had to be confirmed by the US Senate. They voted her in unanimously. In her new job, Lynch directed a team of 178 federal prosecutors, deciding which cases to pursue and how to pursue them.

Lynch's boss, Zachary Carter, retired during the Louima case.

Over the next few months, Lynch told New York mayor Rudy Giuliani that because of the police department's civil rights violations, it would need to be monitored by a federal program. When Giuliani refused, she threatened to bring a lawsuit against the city. The mayor was stunned and angered by this bold move.

New York mayor Rudy Giuliani was angry over Lynch's threat of a lawsuit in light of the NYPD's civil rights violations.

Although she didn't sue the city, the threat was another sign that Lynch would fight for the rights of regular Americans. Over the next couple of years, she also prosecuted Colombian drug lords operating in her jurisdiction, international human traffickers, and corrupt politicians. She gained a reputation for taking on—and winning—big cases.

As usual, she stayed at the office all hours of the day. When her dad came to visit, he often didn't get to see her until late at night. "She worked all the time," he said later. "I was concerned, but I decided to keep my mouth shut."

Even though Lynch was an important public official, she still faced some of the same racial prejudice she had when she was younger. Once, when she was in court, a juror thought she was the defendant in the case. The juror didn't expect to see a black woman with such an important job.

Later, she looked back on what it was like to be a black female US attorney. She said, "I am sure that a long line of dead white men rolled over in their graves. But at the same time, I am sure that just a stone's throw away from here, in the African Burial Ground, a long line of people for whom the law was an instrument of oppression sat up and smiled."

FROM PUBLIC LIFE TO PRIVATE—
AND BACK AGAIN

When Clinton's term ended, Lynch was asked to step down from her role so the new president, George W. Bush, could appoint someone. Lynch returned to practicing law as a partner at a private firm, where she specialized in defending white-collar criminals, or professionals who commit nonviolent financial crimes.

She also began to work pro bono (for free) for the International Criminal Tribunal for Rwanda. This group was established to prosecute people who committed human rights violations during the 1994 tribal genocide in Rwanda. During the summer of 2005, Lynch went to East Africa to interview genocide survivors. Many of them had seen their entire families killed. Her interviews

Dennis Byron, president of the International Criminal Tribunal for Rwanda (*left*), speaks at a United Nations Security Council meeting in 2008.

helped convict the victims' tormentors. She said the work was overwhelming but rewarding.

During this time, she met Stephen Hargrove and began dating him. Hargrove was a master control operator for the cable network Showtime. After they'd been dating for a while, she brought him home to Durham to meet her parents. Lorenzo Lynch Sr. and Hargrove went out for a drive one afternoon, and Hargrove asked for her father's permission to marry her. "I couldn't give you my daughter if I wanted to," her father said. "She's a very independent agent."

Lynch and Hargrove married in 2007, making Lynch the stepmother to Hargrove's two children, Ryan and Kia. That sweet event in her personal life was followed

Lynch married Stephen Hargrove, who is pictured here at a ceremony honoring Lynch's work.

by a tragic one a couple of years later. Her older brother, Lorenzo Lynch Jr., died at the age of fifty-one of diabetes. Losing her big brother at such a young age was a terrible blow for Lynch.

In 2010 the office of US attorney for the Eastern District of New York opened up once again. New York senator Charles Schumer recommended that President Barack Obama nominate Loretta Lynch. "She did an amazing job the first time," Schumer said. "When she handled cases where there was tension between police and the community, both the police and the minority community would go away raving about her. Everyone said she was fair and would always listen." Schumer talked to Lynch about the job. "Your community, your state, your country needs you," he told her.

Obama agreed with Schumer's recommendation and nominated Lynch for a second stint. Once again, the US Senate confirmed her unanimously.

Lynch's focus as US attorney the second time around was a little different from the first. By now, the Colombian drug cartels were no longer a threat. Terrorist organizations like al-Qaeda were the major concern. One US department that she'd be working with a lot—the Department of Homeland Security—hadn't even existed when she held the job the first time.

Lynch's office also continued to go after organized crime. In January 2011, she presided over a massive Mafia bust, arresting 127 members of organized crime families on charges of racketeering, or activity that aids crime

organizations, among other crimes. It was the largest
Mafia bust in New York City history.

Lynch was also in charge of prosecuting a famous case
that had been under investigation for more than three
decades. It involved a daring, high-profile robbery of a
vault at New York's John F. Kennedy International Airport.

On December 11, 1978, several masked mobsters had
forced their way into a secure area of the airport and

Masked mobsters broke into a secure area of New York's John F. Kennedy
International Airport (*below*) in December 1978.

Mobster Jimmy Burke (*center*) is arrested for crimes he committed after the 1978 robbery at the JFK Airport.

tied up ten employees of the German airline Lufthansa. The mobsters forced a worker to open a double vault that contained money and jewels that had been flown over from Germany. The crooks got away with about $5 million in cash and another $1 million in jewels and gold.

The FBI figured out that it was a local organized crime family that was responsible, but they couldn't get enough evidence to arrest anyone. The mastermind of the heist, Jimmy Burke, murdered several of his own crew members so nobody could identify him. Burke was later convicted of other crimes, including one murder, but nobody had been convicted in connection with the Lufthansa robbery.

But in 2011, a former mobster wore a wiretap to visits with Vincent Asaro, a Mafia captain who was connected with the robbery. In recorded conversations, Asaro admitted his part in the robbery.

Mafia captain Vincent Asaro is escorted from FBI offices in Manhattan.

Though many might fear for their lives if they fought the Mafia, Lynch took the case. In January 2014, Asaro was charged for his crimes. It was a sweet victory for Lynch and her office as well as the FBI and everyone who had waited thirty-five years to put the case to rest.

THE PATH TO ATTORNEY GENERAL

Since she worked long hours, Lynch did not have much time for socializing. But she stayed close with her friend from Harvard, Sharon Malone. Malone's husband, Eric Holder, was confirmed as the US attorney general in 2009. Malone and Holder were very familiar with Lynch's great work over the years. Holder appointed Lynch as a member and later the chair of the Attorney General's Advisory Committee. This group helps set policy across all US attorneys' offices.

Meanwhile, Lynch's office continued its fight on behalf of regular Americans. She especially reached out to Muslim Americans, who often face bigotry. "What I hear them saying is what so many African Americans said in the '50s and '60s: 'We're part of America too. We're just like you,'" Lynch said.

At the same time, she did not give up her focus on international issues. She convicted many international terrorism cases, including a 2012 case against an al-Qaeda operative. The man was apparently just days away from a bombing attack on the New York City subway system before he was apprehended.

Lynch was not afraid to go after criminals in powerful positions—including politicians and world leaders. She investigated a money laundering case against an ally of Vladimir Putin, the Russian president. She has sent to jail numerous American politicians for fraud and corruption, including New York representative Michael Grimm, who once worked as an undercover FBI agent. Grimm was accused of wire and mail fraud, filing false tax returns, and other crimes. "Michael Grimm made the choice to go from upholding the law to breaking it," Lynch said.

Investigators made a crack in the FIFA corruption

case around dinnertime on an evening in November 2011 in New York City. A large, well-dressed man was riding a motorized scooter down the sidewalk on Fifth Avenue in Manhattan, on his way to dinner. Behind him trailed two federal agents—one from the FBI and the other from the IRS.

The man's name was Chuck Blazer. He was a former member of the FIFA Executive Committee who had been enjoying the perks of that position for a long time, including taking millions of dollars in bribes and misallocating funds. He'd also avoided paying taxes for close to a decade, which is what finally got him caught. When the federal agents stopped his scooter in the fancy Manhattan neighborhood, they gave him a choice: help the feds bust FIFA officials for widespread corruption or go to prison.

Blazer agreed to help. At the 2012 Olympic Games, he carried a key chain with a microphone in it. He

Former FIFA Executive Committee member Chuck Blazer

FIFA Executive Committee members hold a meeting in a conference room at the La Mamounia Hotel in Morocco in 2014.

met with many FIFA officials and got them to talk about their crimes. It was caught on audio. Over the next few years, Loretta Lynch and her prosecutors' team continued collecting evidence and building their case against the FIFA bosses.

A HARD-WON CONFIRMATION

In 2014 the president of the United States once again noticed Lynch's hard work and stellar reputation. Attorney General Eric Holder was resigning from his position, and on November 8, Barack Obama nominated Lynch to replace him. In a speech with Lynch and Holder by his side, Obama said, "It's pretty hard to be more qualified for this job than Loretta Lynch." He added, "Loretta has spent her life fighting for fair and equal justice that is the foundation of our democracy. I can think of no better public servant to be our next attorney general." Sitting in the audience while the president spoke were several members of her family—her younger brother, Leonzo Lynch, and Stephen Hargrove and his two children. That made the nomination especially meaningful to Lynch.

Lynch and President Barack Obama address members of the news media about counterterrorism legislation.

When it was Lynch's turn to speak, she said, "If I have the honor of being confirmed by the Senate, I will wake up every morning with the protection of the American people my first thought. And I will work every day to safeguard our citizens, our liberties, our rights, and this great nation, which has given so much to me and my family."

Obama pointed out that Lynch had been unanimously confirmed by the US Senate for both her previous federal appointments. He hoped that the Senate would do the same thing again. But as it turned out, a quick confirmation was not going to happen. Republicans and Democrats in the Senate had been fighting over details in an anti-human trafficking bill. Republicans refused to vote on Lynch until the issue was settled.

Senate votes can often get bogged down in political fighting. But Lynch's confirmation turned out to be tenser—and more delayed—than usual. As the weeks went by and still the Senate had not voted, some people criticized Republicans for holding it up. They suggested that racism, sexism, or simple politics—wanting to get back at Obama for actions he'd taken on immigration—might be behind the delay.

Meanwhile, senators grilled Lynch with questions about dozens of issues—including immigration. When she said she essentially agreed with Obama's views on that subject, many Republicans vowed to vote against her. Obama was publicly frustrated. "There are times where the dysfunction in the Senate just goes too far," the president said. "This is an example of it."

While Lynch and Obama waited for confirmation, another issue came up having to do with Lynch's main concern—protecting the rights of all Americans. The United States became gripped by racial turmoil. In August an unarmed young black man named Michael Brown had been shot to death by a white police officer in Ferguson, Missouri. When the officer was not indicted on any charges, protests broke out—first in Ferguson and then in cities across the country. Many viewed the fact

Demonstrators took to the streets of Ferguson, Missouri, to protest the court's decision in the Michael Brown case.

that the officer got away without a trial as a reminder of the abuse minorities often suffer at the hands of police. They said the federal and local governments as well as the police and justice system of this country routinely discriminate against minorities. Michael Brown was just another example. Because his image and story were easy to spread on social media, he became a symbol of the abuse and injustice.

Similar stories began to spread. A twelve-year-old African American boy named Tamir Rice was shot to death by white police in Cleveland. He was unarmed, playing in a park. An African American named Eric Garner died after being put in a choke hold by white police in New York for selling loose cigarettes.

Lynch kept doing her job as US attorney for the Eastern District of New York, which included putting finishing touches on the FIFA charges. Finally, in mid-April 2015, word came that the anti-human-trafficking bill was going to be settled. Lynch's confirmation vote would be coming soon. In North Carolina, eighty-two-year-old Lorenzo Lynch loaded his car and with a friend began to drive to Washington, DC, to witness the vote. He sat in the Senate chamber on April 23 while the senators cast their votes. Lynch was confirmed by a comfortable margin of 56–43.

That same month, a black man named Freddie Gray was arrested in Baltimore, beaten by police, and later died of his injuries. Citizens' outrage over police brutality was inflamed once again. Many protested.

Protesters march in Baltimore to protest the violent circumstances that caused Freddie Gray's death.

Baltimore and the entire country seemed demoralized by yet another story of the murder of a black man by white police.

Though she'd been attorney general for only a short time, Lynch did not hesitate to take a stand on the situation. She visited Baltimore and met with protesters, community leaders, and city officials. She also met with police, many of whom had been working overtime during the protests to protect people's lives and property. She said the death of Freddie Gray and the resulting protests had made her sad. She felt great sympathy for the protesters who, she said, were reeling from "years of anger" and "generations of mistrust."

On May 8, she announced that the Department of Justice would investigate the Baltimore Police Department due to a "serious erosion of public trust." The investigation would seek to find out if the police routinely violated people's rights and were discriminatory. Already, six Baltimore police officers had been charged with crimes connected to Freddie Gray's death, including unlawful imprisonment and murder.

The investigation could not undo the death of Freddie Gray. It could not erase generations of discrimination and pain for minorities in the United States. But it was another battle, like many Lynch had fought in her life, on behalf of ordinary people—people who don't always have the power to fight for themselves. Given Lynch's unfailing work ethic and tireless quest to stand up for the little guy, it seems likely that many such battles are in store for her in the future.

IMPORTANT DATES

1959   Loretta Lynch is born on May 21 in Greensboro, North Carolina.

1965   Her family moves to Durham, North Carolina. Her test results are questioned by white teachers.

1973   She helps with her father's campaign for mayor of Durham.

1977   She graduates from high school.

1981   She graduates from Harvard with an English degree.

1984   She graduates from Harvard Law School and gets a job at a New York law firm.

1990   She begins working for the US attorney's office in the Eastern District of New York.

1994   She is named chief of the Long Island office.

1998   She becomes chief assistant to US attorney Zachary Carter.

1999 She takes a leading role on the trial team that prosecutes and convicts four New York City police officers for violating the civil rights of Haitian immigrant Abner Louima. She is appointed by President Bill Clinton to be the US attorney for the Eastern District of New York.

2005 She serves as special counsel to the prosecutor at the International Criminal Tribunal for Rwanda.

2007 She marries Stephen Hargrove.

2010 She is again nominated to be the US attorney for the Eastern District of New York, this time by President Barack Obama.

2014 Obama nominates Lynch to be the next US attorney general.

2015 She is confirmed by the Senate, 56–43, to be the new US attorney general. After only a short time in office, she levels top FIFA officials with corruption charges.

SOURCE NOTES

9   The United States Attorneys Office—Eastern District of New York,
     "Nine FIFA Officials and Five Corporate Executives Indicted for
     Racketeering Conspiracy and Corruption," news release, May 27,
     2015, http://www.justice.gov/usao/nye/pr/May15/2015
     -May-27.php.

9   Tom McCarthy, "For Loretta Lynch, Fifa Is Just the Latest in a
     String of Tough Targets," *Guardian* (Manchester), May 29, 2015,
     http://www.theguardian.com/us-news/2015/may/29/loretta-lynch
     -profile-fifa-corruption-charges.

11   Josh Gerstein, "For Loretta Lynch, a Stunning Debut on the
     World Stage," *Politico*, May 27, 2015, http://www.politico.com
     /story/2015/05/loretta-lynch-stunning-debut-fifa-soccer-118353
     .html#ixzz3c5tfCkXL.

13   Stephanie Clifford, "Loretta Lynch, a Nominee for Attorney
     General, Is Praised for Substance, Not Flash," *New York Times*,
     November 8, 2014, http://www.nytimes.com/2014/11/09/us
     /politics/in-line-to-be-attorney-general-loretta-lynch-at-home-in
     glare.html?_r=0.

15   "Attorneys at the Top," *Network Journal*, accessed September 2,
     2015, http://www.tnj.com/archives/2007/december
     _jan2008/decjan08issue/cs_decjan08_llynch.php.

18   Ed Stourton, "Loretta Lynch: The Woman 'to Restore Faith in US
     Justice,'" *BBC News*, May 7, 2015, http://www.bbc.com/news
     /world-us-canada-32587698.

19   Seth Stern, "Prosecutor with a Calling," *Harvard Law Today*,
     April 23, 2015, http://today.law.harvard.edu/feature/prosecutor
     -with-a-calling-loretta-lynch-84-becomes-83rd-attorney
     -general-of-the-united-states/.

22   Stourton, "Loretta Lynch."

22   Clifford, "Loretta Lynch."

24 Sari Horwitz, "After Forging Her Path from N.C. to Brooklyn, Lynch Is Poised to Become Attorney General," *Washington Post*, January 26, 2015, http://www.washingtonpost.com/world/national -security/after-forging-her-path-from-nc-to-brooklyn-lynch-is -poised-to-become-attorney-general/2015/01/26/91804eba-a301 -11e4-9f89-561284a573f8_story.html.

24 Stern, "Prosecutor with a Calling."

26 Horwitz, "After Forging Her Path."

27 Ibid.

31 Stern, "Prosecutor with a Calling."

31 Carrie Johnson, "Brooklyn Prosecutor Could Be Nominated Attorney General in Coming Days," *North Country Public Radio*, November 6, 2014, http://www.northcountrypublicradio.org /news/npr/362086721/brooklyn-prosecutor-could-be-nominated -attorney-general-in-coming-days.

34 Evan Perez and Ray Sanchez, "President Nominates Loretta Lynch as Attorney General," *CNN*, November 8, 2014, http://www.cnn.com/2014/11/08/politics/attorney-general -nominee-loretta-lynch/.

34 Anne Blythe, "Loretta Lynch: From Durham to Washington, a Quiet, Effective Career," *Charlotte Observer*, November 15, 2014, http://www.charlotteobserver.com/news/local/article9230072 .html#storylink=cpy.

35 Ibid.

36 "Senate Deal on Trafficking Clears Way for Loretta Lynch Vote," NBC News, April 24, 2015, http://www.nbcnews.com/news /us-news/senate-trafficking-deal-clears-way-loretta-lynch -vote-n345481.

39 Adam Howard, "Loretta Lynch Launches Federal Investigation into Baltimore Police," *MSNBC*, May 8, 2015, http://www .msnbc.com/msnbc/loretta-lynch-launches-federal-investigation -baltimore-police-dept.

39 Ibid.

SELECTED BIBLIOGRAPHY

Blythe, Anne. "Loretta Lynch: From Durham to Washington, a Quiet, Effective Career." *Charlotte Observer*, November 15, 2014. http://www.charlotteobserver.com/news/politics-government/article9232778.html.

Clifford, Stephanie. "Loretta Lynch, a Nominee for Attorney General, Is Praised for Substance, Not Flash." *New York Times*, November 8, 2014. http://www.nytimes.com/2014/11/09/us/politics/in-line-to-be-attorney-general-loretta-lynch-at-home-in-glare.html?_r=0.

Gerstein, Josh. "For Loretta Lynch, a Stunning Debut on the World Stage." *Politico*, May 27, 2015. http://www.politico.com/story/2015/05/loretta-lynch-stunning-debut-fifa-soccer-118353.html#ixzz3c5tfCkXL.

Hirsh, Michael. "What Made Loretta Lynch's Father See Red." *Politico*, April 23, 2015. http://www.politico.com/story/2015/04/what-made-loretta-lynchs-father-see-red-117308.html.

Perez, Evan, and Ray Sanchez. "President Nominates Loretta Lynch as Attorney General." *CNN*, November 8, 2014. http://www.cnn.com/2014/11/08/politics/attorney-general-nominee-loretta-lynch/.

Roberts, Dan. "Fifa Arrests: How a Well-Placed Insider and Stashed Cash Helped US Build Case." *Guardian* (Manchester), May 27, 2015. http://www.theguardian.com/football/2015/may/27/fifa-arrests-corruption-loretta-lynch-chuck-blazer.

"Senate Deal on Trafficking Clears Way for Loretta Lynch Vote." *NBC News*, April 24, 2015. http://www.nbcnews.com/news/us-news/senate-trafficking-deal-clears-way-loretta-lynch-vote-n345481.

Silver, Vernon, Corinne Gretler, and Hugo Miller. "FIFA Busts at Baur au Lac: Inside the Five-Star Takedown." *Bloomberg Business*, May 27, 2015. http://www.bloomberg.com/news/articles/2015-05-27/fifa -busts-at-baur-au-lac-inside-soccer-s-five-star-takedown.

Stern, Seth. "Prosecutor with a Calling." *Harvard Law Today*, April 23, 2015. http://today.law.harvard.edu/feature/prosecutor-with-a-calling -loretta-lynch-84-becomes-83rd-attorney-general-of-the-united -states/.

Stourton, Ed. "Loretta Lynch: The Woman 'to Restore Faith in US Justice.'" *BBC News*, May 7, 2015. http://www.bbc.com/news/world -us-canada-32587698.

FURTHER READING

BOOKS

Hardy, Sheila Jackson, and P. Stephen Hardy. *Extraordinary People of the Civil Rights Movement*. New York: Children's Press, 2007. This book profiles dozens of leaders in the civil rights movement, including the Greensboro Four, who sat down to have lunch at a whites-only counter in Loretta Lynch's hometown.

Krensky, Stephen. *Barack Obama*. New York: DK, 2010. This book tells the story of the United States' first black president.

Landau, Elaine. *The President, Vice President, and Cabinet: A Look at the Executive Branch*. Minneapolis: Lerner Publications, 2012. This book explains what the executive branch is and what it does.

WEBSITES

PBS. "Freedom Riders."
http://ec2-184-73-203-128.compute-1.amazonaws.com/wgbh
/americanexperience/freedomriders
The website for the movie *Freedom Riders*, this page describes the struggle for civil rights in the United States. In addition to summaries of events and key people, it includes video, an interactive map, a timeline, and more.

The United States Department of Justice: Office of the Attorney General
http://www.justice.gov/ag
The online home of the attorney general's office contains current news as well as history and a complete list of past attorneys general.

INDEX

PHOTO ACKNOWLEDGMENTS

The images in this book are used with the permission of: © Chip Somodevilla/ Getty Images, pp. 2, 34; © Bill Clark/CQ Roll Call/Getty Images, p. 6; Darren Fletcher Photography Limited/Newscom, p. 8; © Pascal Mora/The New York Times/Redux, p. 9; © Spencer Platt/Getty Images, p. 10; © Everett Collection Historical/Alamy, p. 12; © Ted Richardson/for The Washington Post via Getty Images, p. 13; © Hulton Archive/Getty Images, p. 14; © Jannis Werner (Harvard Images)/Alamy, p. 17; © Andrew Savulich/NY Daily News Archive via Getty Images, p. 20; AP Photo/Todd Plitt, p. 21; © Robert Rosamilio/NY Daily News Archive via Getty Image, p. 23; © Albert H. Teich/Shutterstock.com, p. 24; © Don Emmert/AFP/Getty Images, p. 25; © EPA/Shawn Thew/Alamy, p. 26; AP Photo/Seth Wenig, p. 28; Thomas Monaster/NY Daily News Archive via Getty Images, p. 29; AP Photo/Newsday/Charles Eckert, p. 30; © Francois-Xavier Marit/ AFP/Getty Images, p. 32; © Ian Walton/FIFA via Getty Images, p. 33; © Scott Olson/Getty Images, p. 36; © Andrew Burton/Getty Images, p. 38.

Cover: © Ramin Talaie/Getty Images.